Kids' Travel Guide
thailand

FlyingKids Presents:
Kids' Travel Guide
thailand

Author: Sarah-Jane Williams

Editor: Carma Graber

Cover Illustrations and design: Francesca Guido

Graphic designer: Neboysha Dolovacki

Published by FlyingKids

Visit us @ www.theflyingkids.com

 Contact us: leonardo@theflyingkids.com

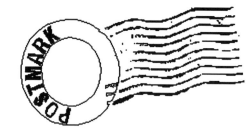

ISBN: 978-1502904225

Acknowledgment:

All images are Dollar Photo Stock or public domain, except those mentioned below:

Diomedia:12mr; CanStockPhoto:15m; Shutterstock: 1bgl, 1bgbr, 11bg, 11ml, , 13bgl, 15bgtl, 17bgt, 17mr, 17bgbr, 18mbcl, 20mr, 21bgcr, 21bgbr, 22bg, 22m, 22bg, 22ml, 22mr, 25bgl, 26m, 26bg, 27bg, 28bg, 29bg, 30bg, 31bg, 31mr, 31ml, 32bgtl, 33bg, 34bg, 35ml, 35bg, 35mbl, 36bgtl, 37ml, 38bg, 39bgr; Attribution: 32m-By David Maiolo (Own work) [CC BY-SA 3.0 (http://creativecommons.org/licenses/by-sa/3.0)], via Wikimedia Commons.

Key: t=top; b=bottom; l=left; r=right; c=center; m=main image; bg=background

table of contents

This is the only page for parents in this book ...

Dear Parents,

If you bought this book, you're probably planning a family trip with your kids. You are spending a lot of time and money in the hopes that this family vacation will be pleasant and fun. You would like your children to learn a little about the country you visit – its geography, history, unique culture, traditions, and more. And you hope they will always remember the trip as a very special experience.

The reality is often quite different. Parents find themselves frustrated as they struggle to convince their kids to join a tour or visit a landmark, while the kids just want to stay in and watch TV. On the road, the children are glued to their mobile devices instead of enjoying the new sights and scenery – or they complain and constantly ask, "When are we going to get there?" Many parents are disappointed after they return home and discover that their kids don't remember much about the trip and the new things they learned.

That's exactly why *Kids' Travel Guide – Thailand* was created.

How does it work?

A family trip is fun. But difficulties can arise when children are not in their natural environment. *Kids' Travel Guide – Thailand* takes this into account and supports children as they get ready for the trip, visit new places, learn new things, and finally, return home.

Kids' Travel Guide – Thailand does this by helping children to prepare for the trip and know what to expect. During the trip, kids will read relevant facts about Thailand and get advice on how to adapt to new situations. The kids will meet Leonardo – their tour guide. Leonardo encourages them to experiment, explore, and be more involved in the family's activities – as well as to learn new information and make memories throughout the trip.

Kids' Travel Guide – Thailand includes puzzles, tasks to complete, useful tips, and other recommendations along the way. In addition, kids are asked to document and write about their experiences during the trip, so that when you return home, they will have a memoir that will be fun to look at and reread again and again.

Kids' Travel Guide – Thailand offers general information about Thailand, so it is useful regardless of the city or part of the country you plan to visit. It includes basic geography; flag, symbols, and coins; basic history; and colorful facts about culture and customs in Thailand. If you are traveling to Bangkok, you may also want to get the *Kids' Travel Guide – Bangkok*, which focuses on the city itself – its history and culture, and all its interesting and unique attractions.

Ready for a new experience?
Have a nice trip and have fun!

Hi, Kids!

If you are reading this book, it means you are lucky –
you are going to **Thailand**!

You probably already know what areas you will visit, and you may
have noticed that your parents are getting ready for the journey. They
have bought travel guides, looked for information on the Internet, and
printed pages of information. They are talking to friends and people
who have already visited **Thailand**, in order to learn about it and know
what to do, where to go, and when … But this is not just another
guidebook for your parents.

THIS BOOK IS FOR YOU ONLY – THE YOUNG TRAVELER.

So what is this book all about?

First and foremost, meet **Leonardo**, your
very own personal guide on this
trip. Leonardo has visited
many places around the
world (guess how he got
there ౨ఠ), and he will be
with you throughout the **book** and the trip.
Leonardo will tell you all about the places you will
visit – it is always good to learn a little bit about the
country and its history beforehand. He will provide
many ideas, quizzes, tips, and other surprises.
Leonardo will accompany you while you are packing and
leaving home. He will stay in the hotel with you (don't worry,
it does not cost more money ౨ఠ)! And he will see the sights
with you until you return home.

A Travel Diary – The Beginning!

Going to thailand!!!

How did you get to Thailand?

By plane / ship / car / other _____

Date of arrival _____ Time _____

Date of departure _____

We will stay in Thailand for _____ days.

Is this your first visit ? yes / no

Where will you sleep? In a hotel / In a campsite / In a motel /

In an apartment / With family / In a guesthouse / Other _____

What places are you planning to visit?

_____

_____

_____

What special activities are you planning to do?

_____

_____

_____

Are you excited about the trip?

This is an excitement indicator. Ask your family members how excited they are (from "not at all" up to "very, very much"), and mark each of their answers on the indicator. Leonardo has already marked the level of his excitement …

not at all — very, very much

Leonardo

Who is
traveling?

Write down the names of the family members traveling with you and their answers to the questions.

Name: _____

Age: _____

Have you visited Thailand before? yes / no

What is the most exciting thing about your upcoming trip?

_____
_____
_____

Name: _____

Age: _____

Have you visited Thailand before? yes / no

What is the most exciting thing about your upcoming trip?

_____
_____
_____

Name: _____

Age: _____

Have you visited Thailand before? yes / no

What is the most exciting thing about your upcoming trip?

_____
_____
_____

Name: _____

Age: _____

Have you visited Thailand before? yes / no

What is the most exciting thing about your upcoming trip?

_____
_____
_____

Name: _____

Age: _____

Have you visited Thailand before? yes / no

What is the most exciting thing about your upcoming trip?

_____
_____
_____

Preparations at home – DO NOT FORGET ...!

Mom or Dad will take care of packing clothes (how many pairs of pants, which comb to take …). Leonardo will only tell you the stuff he thinks you might want to bring along on your trip to Thailand.

Leonardo made a Packing List for you. Check off each item as you pack it!

☐ *Kids' Travel Guide – **Thailand** – of course* ☺
☐ Comfortable walking shoes
☐ A raincoat or umbrella (sometimes it rains without warning)
☐ A hat (and sunglasses, if you want)
☐ Pens and pencils
☐ Crayons and markers (It is always nice to color and paint.)
☐ A book to read
☐ Your smartphone/tablet or camera

Pack your things in a small bag (or backpack).

You may also want to take these things:

Snacks, fruit, candy, and chewing gum. If you are flying, chewing gum can help a lot during takeoff and landing, when there's pressure in your ears.

Games you can play while sitting down: electronic games, booklets of crossword puzzles, connect-the-numbers (or connect-the-dots), etc.

Remember to take a notebook or a writing pad. You can use it for games, writing, or to draw or doodle in when you are bored …

 Now let's see if you can find 12 items you should take on a trip in this Word search puzzle:

☐ Leonardo
☐ walking shoes
☐ hat
☐ raincoat
☐ crayons
☐ book
☐ pencil
☐ camera
☐ snacks
☐ fruit
☐ patience
☐ good mood

P	A	T	I	E	N	C	E	A	W	F	G
E	L	R	T	S	G	Y	J	W	A	T	O
Q	E	Y	U	Y	K	Z	K	M	L	W	O
H	O	S	N	A	S	N	Y	S	K	G	D
A	N	R	Z	C	P	E	N	C	I	L	M
C	A	M	E	R	A	A	W	G	N	E	O
R	R	A	I	N	C	O	A	T	G	Q	O
Y	D	S	G	I	R	K	Z	K	S	H	D
S	O	A	C	O	A	E	T	K	H	A	T
F	R	U	I	T	Y	Q	O	V	O	D	A
B	O	O	K	F	O	H	Z	K	E	R	T
T	K	Z	K	A	N	S	I	E	S	Y	U
O	V	I	E	S	S	N	A	C	K	S	P

Let's meet Thailand – the land of smiles!

Thailand is one of the most popular countries in Southeast Asia. The friendly people are always smiling – so its nickname is the **Land of Smiles**! Many Thais say that Thailand means **Land of the Free**.

Around **20 million** people visit Thailand each year. In Thailand, you can enjoy gorgeous **beaches** and **islands**, climb in the cool **mountains**, see lots of wildlife, visit really old, sparkling **temples**, walk around lively **cities**, take it easy in quiet **villages**, eat delicious **food** … and more!

Leonardo can't wait to tell you all about this great country. Let's get started …

Do you know what continent Thailand is on?

Answer: Asia

How many words can you make from "Land of Smiles"? (example: sand)

_____

_____

_____

_____

_____

_____

_____

Did you know?
There is one place in Thailand where the weather can be freezing! The temperatures can reach 0 degrees Celsius (32 degrees Fahrenheit) in Loei Province.

Thailand is known as the Land of …
a) Beaches
b) Sun
c) Smiles
d) Rice

Answer: Smiles!

thailand
on the map

ราชอาณาจักรไทย

THAILAND

Where is **Thailand** on the map?
Can you point out **Thailand**?
Go over **Thailand's borders** and
mark them.

What is a compass rose?

The compass rose is a drawing that shows the directions: North-South-East-West. North is always at the top of the map, and from that you can find the other directions. When you need to get to a place, you can use a compass. A compass rose is drawn on the face of the compass, and the needle always points North. This helps you to navigate and figure out what direction to go – so you can get from one place to another.

Write down the three missing directions in the blank squares.

North

MYANMAR
LAOS
CAMBODIA
Andaman Sea
Gulf of Thailand
MALAYSIA

Many people say Thailand looks like an elephant's head – can you see it 👀?

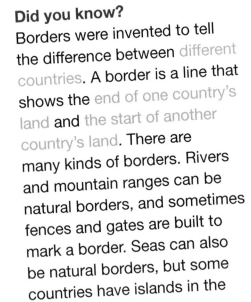

Did you know?
Borders were invented to tell the difference between different countries. A border is a line that shows the end of one country's land and the start of another country's land. There are many kinds of borders. Rivers and mountain ranges can be natural borders, and sometimes fences and gates are built to mark a border. Seas can also be natural borders, but some countries have islands in the ocean.

Thailand is surrounded by several neighboring countries and seas. Can you find them on the map?

To the North _____

To the South _____

To the East _____

To the West _____

Answers:
Myanmar (Burma), Laos
Malaysia
Cambodia, Laos, Gulf of Thailand
Myanmar (Burma), Andaman Sea

Let's have a look at thailand's main cities ...

Help Leonardo to find these 10 cities:

- ☐ Bangkok
- ☐ Phuket
- ☐ Chiang Mai
- ☐ Chiang Rai
- ☐ Rangsit
- ☐ Ayutthaya
- ☐ Pattaya
- ☐ Lampang
- ☐ Rayong
- ☐ Trang

L	C	E	H	A	T	B	U	S	D
A	Y	U	T	T	H	A	Y	A	I
M	N	P	U	R	T	N	P	P	E
P	C	H	I	A	N	G	M	A	I
A	K	U	A	Y	B	K	D	T	R
N	E	K	I	O	R	O	G	T	A
G	C	E	D	N	A	K	R	A	L
X	M	T	O	G	C	A	H	Y	I
V	C	H	I	A	N	G	R	A	I
R	T	I	S	G	N	A	R	M	N

Do you know what a province is? Each country is split into different parts. These parts may be called counties, states, regions, or provinces. In Thailand, there are 77 provinces.

Did you know?
There is a joke that Thailand actually has 78 provinces – with the last province located in Los Angeles, California, USA. This is because of the large Thai population living there.

Let's have a look at **Thailand's main cities** …

ธตกgkok – capital city

Thailand's capital city of **Bangkok** is home to around 14 million people, making it the biggest city in Thailand.

It has the longest place name in the world! In Thai, the city's full name is:

Krungthepmahanakhon Amonrattanakosin Mahintharayutthaya Mahadilokphop Noppharatratchathaniburirom Udomratchaniwetmahasathan Amonphimanawatansathit Sakkathattiyawitsanukamprasit

Try to say it 😊 !

Luckily the nickname is much easier – **The City of Angels.**

There are lots of **historical buildings** in Bangkok, such as the Grand Palace, the Temple of the Emerald Buddha, Wat Arun, and Wat Pho. There are normal **markets** and floating markets, **parks**, many **museums**, and a **zoo**. You can also take **boat trips** on the river and canals.

Did you know?
In Thai, *wat* means "temple."

Quizzes!

1. What kind of markets are there?

_____

2. What is Bangkok's nickname?

_____

3. You can take boat trips on the river and

_____

Answers:
1. Normal and floating
2. The City of Angels
3. Canals

Phuket –
picture-perfect beaches

The city of Phuket is Thailand's biggest island – but because it is so big, it is easy to forget that you are on an island! It is joined to the mainland by a road, so you don't need a boat to get there.

Phuket is famous for its stunning beaches. You can find those that are very busy and energetic as well as those that are quiet and peaceful. There are also lots of things to do away from the white sandy beaches – temples, **scenic views, shows, nature safaris, waterfalls,** elephant rides, a crocodile farm … and more!

Can you see Phuket on the map? (Clue: it's near the South.)

What sea surrounds Phuket?

Answer: Andaman Sea

The sea around Phuket is home to corals, underwater rock formations, small sharks, eels, rays, crabs, turtles, and lots of brightly colored fish!

Draw your favorite sea creature:

chiang Mai -
the cultural capital

Found in the North, Chiang Mai is often said to be the cultural capital of Thailand. It is also one of the best places for nature, scenery, and wildlife.

Chiang Mai is home to over 500 gleaming temples, as well as several elephant camps, where you can get up close and personal with these magnificent creatures. It has many beautiful waterfalls – plus the **jungle** is very close to the city.

The highest place in Thailand is close to the city of Chiang Mai, and it is called **Doi Inthanon**. The temperature is usually lower in Chiang Mai because it is close to the mountains.

Did you know?

There are several different ethnic groups, often called "hill tribes," that live near to Chiang Mai. They often wear traditional clothes and make handicrafts.

Does your country have a traditional costume?
If so, what does it look like?

Do you know the differences between an Asian elephant and an African elephant?
• Asian elephants are smaller.
• Asian elephants have smaller ears.
• All African elephants have tusks – only some male Asian elephants have them.
• The heads, teeth, skin, trunks, and toenails are different!

Now, take a look at the pictures ... which one is Asian and which one is African 👀?

Ayutthaya – the ancient kingdom

Ayutthaya was once a powerful kingdom, long before present-day Thailand's borders were created. It is surrounded by rivers and canals, so it's sometimes called an island. In the past, it was often referred to as "The Venice of the East." There are many old temple ruins – close your eyes and imagine how grand they must have looked many years ago!

The kingdom was ruined when Burmese invaders ransacked the city. They also chopped the heads off many of the Buddha statues, so most statues you see today are headless!

Ayutthaya is famous for the sweet snack "Roti Sai Mai." It is like candy floss wrapped in a crepe.

Look for the famous Buddha head in a tree and take a picture.

Here's a temple for you to color. Write a word in the cloud to describe Ayutthaya.

Flag and symbols

This is the flag of Thailand.

As you can see, the flag has three colors – **red**, white, and **blue**. Each color has a meaning:

Red represents the people and the nation.
White represents the Buddhist religion.
Blue is for the Royal Family.

This is the **symbol of Thailand**. It has been the national symbol since 1911, but was used long before this time.

It is a mythical bird called a **Garuda**.

The creature has the face, beak, wings, legs, and claws of a bird, but it has the body of what? Look closely!

Answer: A (male) person

Other symbols of Thailand are:
Asian elephant (National animal)
Thai Pavilion (National building)
Flower from the golden shower tree (National flower)

Which is NOT a symbol of Thailand? Mark ✓ or X ...

Answer: Monkey

How to buy stuff in thailand

The type of money that a country uses is called the currency. The currency in Thailand is the Thai baht. Thailand is the only country that uses the Thai baht.

There are 100 satang in 1 baht – although satangs are so small that many places will not accept them! You will see most prices rounded to the nearest whole baht.

There are notes and coins. The notes come in amounts of 1,000 baht, 500 baht, 100 baht, 50 baht, and 20 baht. All notes have an image of the current king. The coins are 10 baht, 5 baht, 2 baht, 1 baht, 50 satang, and 25 satang. The king's head is on one side of all coins.

In some places, especially markets in tourist areas, bartering and haggling may be expected. This is where the buyer and seller negotiate a price. Don't be surprised if you are asked how much you will pay for something rather than being told a fixed price !

Quizzes!

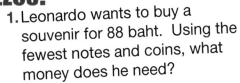

What is on the back of a 10 baht coin?
A bird
A temple
A tree
A person

Answer: A temple

Did you know?
Because the king is very special in Thailand, it is against the law to stand on anything that shows his picture. So, it is illegal to step on Thai money!

1. Leonardo wants to buy a souvenir for 88 baht. Using the fewest notes and coins, what money does he need?

_____

2. What is the smallest note?

_____

3. What is the largest coin?

_____

4. If Leonardo buys a bag for 150 baht and a pencil for 75 baht, how much change will he get if he pays with a 500 baht note?

_____

Answer: **1.** 50, 20, 10, 5, 2, and 1 baht **2.** 20 baht **3.** 10 baht **4.** 275 baht

History: kingdoms and conflicts!

Thai people originally lived in the southern parts of China. They moved down into the area that is now Thailand over many, many years!

Before Thailand became the country it is today, there were several powerful kingdoms. These included the Kingdoms of Lanna, Sukhothai, Ayutthaya, Thonburi, and Bangkok.

Ayutthaya was one of the most powerful kingdoms, and it controlled lots of land. **Burmese** forces invaded the kingdom in the 1750s and 1760s and eventually conquered the city. The final King of Ayutthaya starved to death after the rest of the royal family had run away!

A new king took control of the situation, and the capital city was moved to Thonburi. A few years later it moved again – just across the river to **Bangkok**. Bangkok has been the capital since 1782.

Europeans used to refer to the country as Siam, although this name was not initially used by Thai people. But it became the official name of the country in 1856, when an agreement was signed with Great Britain. In 1939 the name was changed to Thailand. Siam was used again between 1945 and 1949, before changing back to Thailand.

Do you know anything about your country's history? Write down some of the main points.

_____

_____

_____

_____

Did you know? Thailand is the only country in Southeast Asia that was never taken over by a European country.

The royal family

Thailand still has a royal family. Until 1932 the royal family ruled the country. A revolution removed many of their royal powers, and Thailand became a "constitutional monarchy." A constitutional monarchy is a country that has a royal family, but a government is in charge of the country – the king and queen do not rule the country.

There have been several **dynasties** in Thailand – where each king is from the same family as the king before.

The present dynasty is called the **Chakri Dynasty**. This dynasty started a long time ago in 1782. The present king is the ninth king in the Chakri Dynasty. His name is **King Bhumibol Adulyadeji**, and he has been the king since 1946. He is the longest-serving monarch in the whole world!

In the past there was a law that prevented regular people from touching a member of the royal family. The punishment was **death**. This caused a tragic event where a queen drowned as people watched – everyone was too afraid to try to help her in case they were punished. This law was then changed.

Quizzes!

What is the name of the dynasty in Thailand today?

_____

What happened to change Thailand to a constitutional monarchy?

_____

What did the former law prevent?

_____

Chakri

Revolution

Touching royalty

Answers:

(Fairly) recent history

Since Thailand became a constitutional monarchy in 1932, all has not been plain sailing. In fact, people have sometimes been so unhappy with the government that there have been protests and demonstrations. The army has tried to take control of the country and remove the government a massive 19 times! This is called a coup. There have been 12 successful coups in Thailand, and the latest was in May 2014.

Have you EVER heard about ASEAN?

Thailand is one of the 10 members of **ASEAN** – the Association of South East Asian Nations. The members try to work together for peace and growth.

Can you complete the names of the other nine ASEAN countries?

Br_n_i
Bu_m_
C_m_o_i
I__o_es_a
L__s
Ma___s_a
Phi_i_pi__s
S___a_o_e
V__t_am

Did you know?
In 2011 Thailand suffered some of the worst flooding it had seen for many years.

Did you know?
The first recorded Siamese twins were born in Thailand in 1811.

But what are Siamese twins?

Siamese twins is another name for conjoined twins – or twins that have not properly separated before being born, and so are joined together! Today, it is possible in many cases to separate Siamese twins with an operation. This was not possible in 1811 though, when the first known case of Siamese twins happened in Thailand. The twins were called Chang and Eng Bunker. They spent their whole lives joined together, although each did get married and have children!

Now let's talk about the Thai people!

Culture and customs

Most Thai children learn English in school … it is easy to make new friends!

Thai people greet each other with the *wai*. This is a combination of a small bow with the hands flat together. It looks a bit like praying. Thais also use the wai to say goodbye, apologize, give thanks, and show respect.

Most Thais are **Buddhist**. Try to spot monks wearing orange robes walking around the streets and temples.

Thais see **feet** as being dirty. You shouldn't point with your feet, especially in a special place. The head is the most important part of the body for Thai people. Be careful not to touch anyone's head!

Did you know?
Thais should keep their heads lower than those of anyone older or more important than them.

Tip!

You will need to take off your shoes to go inside many places in Thailand. Wear shoes that are quick and easy to take off and put back on – you don't want to be tying your laces every five minutes!

Family is very important in Thailand. Many extended families live close together in the same village or town. Large families usually meet up for celebrations and holidays.

Look around you … can you help Leonardo to find more Thai customs?

_____

_____

_____

Bon Appetit!

Thai cuisine (cooking)

The main food in Thailand is rice. It is eaten at almost every meal, and can be served with a variety of other dishes. Noodles and **soups** are also popular.

Thai food is known for being very spicy – look out! Cucumber is often served with spicy meals, as it helps to cool the mouth.

One of the most famous dishes in Thailand is Pad Thai. This is stir-fried noodles with egg and tofu. It may also contain peanuts, bean sprouts, prawns, or chicken. The flavor comes from fish sauce and tamarind – a type of tangy fruit.

Fried rice is also well-known. It may contain vegetables, pork, chicken, seafood, or egg.

Som Tam is another favorite. It originated in the eastern part of Thailand. It is a spicy papaya salad.

What's your favorite food from your country? _____

What's your favorite Thai food? _____

Make a list of all the Thai foods you have tasted:

_____
_____
_____
_____

Bon Appetit!

Did you know?
Thais usually eat with a fork and a spoon. Knives are not usually used. Chopsticks are often used for noodle dishes.

Have you used chopsticks to eat?

Eating bugs … !
Some Thais eat bugs as snacks! Bugs can include crickets, beetles, and worms!

Would you try a bug?!

Tasty fruits
There are also lots of yummy and exotic fruits in Thailand – such as the pink and spiky dragon fruit and the hairy-looking rambutin. The durian fruit is known for being really smelly!

What's your favorite fruit?

Can you guess what's bubbling in the pot?

(The Thai name is *Tom Yam Gung*.)

a. Rice
b. Stew
c. Noodles
d. Fried Egg
e. Soup
f. Pizza

Answer: e. Soup!

Don't be scared to try new foods. Many may look different, but most are delicious!

(25)

Bon Appetit!

Besides restaurants, markets are a popular place for Thai people to buy food. Your family can buy fresh meals as well as different ingredients, and some stalls have seating areas for customers. Others only do meals to take away.

Street food is a HUGE concept in Thailand – you will see lots of food sellers all over the place. Indeed, you will never be too far away from a place to buy a snack or a full meal!

It is VERY difficult to go hungry in Thailand!

Many people joke that eating is almost a pastime of Thais – most like to eat little and often, and will snack throughout the day.

 Take a picture of your favorite Thai meal.

Draw on the plate what you ate for dinner last night.

Did you know?
When a group of Thai people sit down to eat together, it is usual for them to share lots of dishes. Individual plates are not so common.

Thai language

The Thai language can be very tricky to learn. It uses its own script / character system and is also a tonal language. There are five tones in Thai. This means that the meaning of a sound can change depending on the tone you use.

The tones are:

Low

Mid

High

Rising

Falling

Try to say your name in the five different tones!

The Thai alphabet has 44 consonants. There are 15 symbols for vowels, but these can be combined to create at least 28 different vowel sounds. There are also four symbols to show different tones.

Did you know?
The spoken languages in Thailand and Laos are very similar.

To be polite, men add the word *krap* at the end of their statements. Females add *ka*.

The word for "I" also depends on whether you are a boy or a girl. Boys refer to themselves as *pomme*. Girls refer to themselves as *chan*.

Are you pomme or chan 😊 ?

Did you know?
The Thai words for "rice," "mountain," "white," and "news" sound very similar to the untrained ear!

This is how you write "Thailand" in Thai:

ประเทศไทย

Now you try … Can you copy it?

27

How do you say in thai...?

Do you want to know a few words and phrases in Thai?
Leonardo will help you with some basics!

And remember – if you are a boy you will finish with *krap*; if you are a girl you will finish with *ka*.

Hello / Goodbye   Sa-wa-dee ka / krap

Thank you   Kap khun ka / krap

Yes   Chai

No   Mai chai

No   Mai ow
(as in you do not want something)

Good   Dee

Bad   Mai dee

My name is ...   Chan / Pomme chur ... ka / krap

Circle and complete:

Chan / Pomme chur _____   ka / krap

Did you know?
Mai before a word shows a negative.
Mai at the end of a sentence makes it a question.

Let's look at numbers!

Symbol in English	Pronunciation in Thai		Symbol in English	Pronunciation in Thai
0	Soon		21	Yee-sip-et
1	Nueng		22	Yee-sip-song
2	Song		23	Yee-sip-sam
3	Sam		24	Yee-sip-see
4	See		25	Yee-sip-ha
5	Ha		…	…
6	Hock		30	Sam-sip
7	Jet		40	See-sip
8	Bat		50	Ha-sip
9	Gow		60	Hock-sip
10	Sip		…	
11	Sip-et		100	Loy
12	Sip-song		200	Song Loy
13	Sip-sam		…	…
14	Sip-see		1,000	Pan
15	Sip-ha			
…	…			
20	Yee-sip			

Practice saying your age in Thai!

How old are your family members? (In Thai!)

In the Restaurant

Here are some handy words and phrases to help you out when ordering food – go on, **try to order** in Thai the next time you go to a restaurant!

English Word	Thai Word	English Word	Thai Word
Rice	Khao	Breakfast	Ahan chow
Egg	Khai	Lunch	Ahan tee-ang
Pork	Moo	Dinner	Ahan yen
Chicken	Gai	Spicy	Pet
Prawn	Gung	Not Spicy	Mai pet
Fish	Blah	Vegetarian	Mang sa wee rat
Vegetable	Pak	Delicious	Aroy
Water	Nam	Restaurant	Rong ahan
Milk	Nom	Food	Ahan

Write the Thai word in the box and color the pictures:

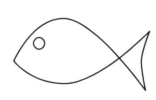

Fun facts

Everyone's interested in the biggest, the smallest, the fastest, the slowest, and the strange and unique things that make a place special, right? So let's have a look at some of these interesting things from Thailand!

- The **highest place** in Thailand is at Doi Inthanon near Chiang Mai. The peak of the mountain stands at 2,565 meters tall (8,415 feet).

- Thailand is home to one of the world's tallest stupas (similar to a pagoda). It is in Nakhorn Pathom, a short way outside of Bangkok. The stupa is just over 120 meters tall (394 feet).

- Thailand's biggest Buddha statue is in Ang Thong. It Is 92 meters tall (302 feet) and Is the ninth largest statue in the world!

- Thailand is the world's biggest exporter of orchid flowers.

- The world's **smallest mammal** lives in Thailand. It is a type of bat.

- Thailand held the most expensive pet wedding in the world! Two rare cats were married in 1996.

- Thailand has over 1,400 islands – but many don't have people living on them!

- A really strange creature that lives in Thailand is the **mudskipper** – it is a fish that can survive on land and climb trees!

- Based on average temperatures, Bangkok is the **hottest** capital city in the whole world!

sports

Many sports are popular in Thailand – football, badminton, volleyball, golf, tennis, squash, and bowling. The long coastline also makes water sports such as diving and snorkeling popular.

Lots of Thai people (males especially!) like to follow European football.

What is your favorite football team? _____

What color is their uniform? _____

There are also some traditional sports that are fairly unique to Thailand:

Thai boxing, also called Muay Thai, is now becoming popular all around the world. But it started in Thailand as a defensive activity – soldiers trained in Thai boxing many years ago. It's different from regular boxing in that fighters can use all parts of their body as both a weapon and a shield. The opening rituals are also exciting and interesting.

Takraw is another traditional sport. It is vaguely similar to volleyball, except a small ball is used and players don't use their hands – they can use their feet, knees, and head to knock the ball over the net.

Elephant polo is pretty unusual – and lots of fun to watch! Competitors ride elephants and try to hit a ball with a stick. It is only played in three countries – Thailand, Sri Lanka, and Nepal.

Did you know?
Since 1952, Thailand has taken part in every Summer Olympics – except for one year. They have only walked away with 21 medals, though, in all those years! Most medals were won in boxing.

Find the sports:
Golf, Boxing, Football, Diving, Polo, Tennis, Takraw, Bowling

Y	M	G	N	I	V	I	D	F
G	N	I	L	W	O	B	O	A
P	E	L	G	O	L	O	P	W
S	I	N	N	E	T	X	S	A
A	N	G	D	B	O	I	R	R
I	H	O	A	C	X	N	A	K
N	A	L	M	S	J	G	W	A
D	L	F	A	T	O	S	E	T

Religion

You already know by now that Buddhism is the main religion in Thailand. Around 95 percent of Thai people are Buddhist.

What is Buddhism?

There are several different forms of Buddhism – the main type in Thailand is called Theravada. Thai Buddhism has big influences from Chinese Buddhism, Hinduism, and ancient beliefs.

Doing good things is a major part of Thai Buddhism. People do this by giving money to the temple, releasing caged birds, giving food to monks, etc. Another key part is a belief that every action has a reaction – if you do good things, good will come back to you. If you do bad things though, you will get bad luck in return. Being reborn again (reincarnation) is another strong principle.

Traditionally, men were expected to become **monks** for a short period of their lives. Many men still do this today. You can recognize monks by their orange robes.

The Thai king must be Buddhist too, and usually spends some time as a monk.

Thai people visit the temples to pray, to make offerings and donations, and to ask for good luck. Monks may sometimes be asked about lucky dates and for basic medical advice.

Ancient beliefs that still exist within modern spiritual practices include a belief in ghosts and spirits. Many buildings have small spirit houses and shrines where food and drink are left as offerings. Wearing amulets (or charms) is also linked to ancient beliefs.

Have you ever visited a temple?
Have you been to a temple in Thailand?

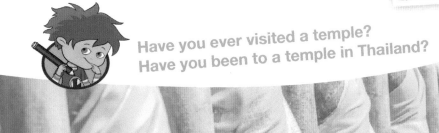

weather and seasons

Thailand has **three** seasons – hot, cool, and wet. The time of year for each season changes depending on the part of the country.

How many seasons are there in your country? _____

Can you name them? _____

What is your favorite season? _____

The hot season is, unsurprisingly, the hottest time of the year! It is often very **sunny** too.

The cool season is rarely very cold – although the temperatures are lower than at other times of the year. It can feel a bit **chilly** at night though, so having a **sweater** is advised! The temperature is also usually lower in the northern parts of the country and in the mountains.

There are lots of storms and **heavy rains** in the wet season, although it can also be very sunny and warm. Some parts of the country regularly have **floods** in the wet season.

What's the weather like today?

_____

_____

_____

Did you know?
You may have noticed traditional wooden houses that are raised on stilts ... Part of the reason for having higher homes is for protection if there are floods!

Take a photo of a traditional Thai home on stilts.

Wildlife

There are lots of different animals and creatures that live in the wild in Thailand. Some are very easy to spot, whereas others are now quite rare.

Some rare animals that roam freely in parts of Thailand include elephants, tigers, bears, crocodiles, and white rhinos. You are VERY unlikely to see any of these in the wild though.

You will see lots of other creatures though!

There are many beautiful birds and butterflies, as well as big snakes, lizards, and other interesting creepy crawlies.

There are plenty of **lizards**, from the small gecko to the large dragon-like monitor lizard. Listen for the loud and distinctive calls of the tokay lizard. Its noise sounds like it is shouting, "Tokay, tokay," over and over again!

There are wild **monkeys** in some places too. Be careful though – the brown ones are known to try to steal things! Keep all food and drink well hidden!

There are deer, bats, fish, turtles, dolphins, whales, squirrels, otters … and much more!

There are lots of dogs and cats that live on the streets in Thailand. Don't touch them – they may bite! The stray animals are often not friendly.

Can you see the spider hiding on the bark 👀?

What do you know about **thailand** 😉?

1. What is Thailand's national animal? _____

2. What is the main food in Thailand? _____

3. What is the main religion in Thailand? _____

4. How many seasons does Thailand have? _____

5. What is the capital city of Thailand? _____

6. What colors are in the Thai flag? _____

7. Is Chiang Mai in the North, South, East, or West? _____

8. What is the currency in Thailand? _____

9. Does Phuket have beaches? (Yes / No) _____

10. How many tones does the Thai language have? _____

11. What type of sport is Muay Thai? _____

12. What city has hill tribes? _____

13. What is Bangkok's nickname? _____

14. Which season has a lot of rain? _____

Answers:
1. (Asian) Elephant
2. Rice
3. Buddhism
4. 3
5. Bangkok
6. Red, white, blue
7. North
8. Thai baht
9. Yes
10. 5
11. Boxing
12. Chiang Mai
13. City of Angels
14. Wet season

Did you know?
In Thailand, each day of the week has an associated color. If you know the day that you were born, you can find out your own Thai color!

Monday	Yellow
Tuesday	Pink
Wednesday	Green
Thursday	Orange
Friday	Light blue
Saturday	Purple
Sunday	Red

The king's color is yellow – what day was he born?

_____

The queen's color is blue – what day was she born?

_____

If Leonardo was born on a **Thursday**, what is his color?

_____

This is your Thai color shirt! Color it for the day you were born.

Answers:
King – Monday
Queen – Friday
Leonardo – Orange

Can you find five differences between the butterflies?

Did you know?
Karaoke is very popular in Thailand. There are even karaoke rooms in many malls!

What's your favorite song?

37

Can you break the code?

Use the key below to figure out Leonardo's journal entry about his trip to Thailand:

J = A Q = R Z = I 9 = S 2 = E 4 = O

I had a fantastic time in THJILJND (_ _ _ _ _ _ _ _)! I loved visiting BJNGK4K
(_ _ _ _ _ _ _) and spending time on the beautiful B2JCH29 (_ _ _ _ _ _ _).
I thought the different T2MPL2S were really interesting, and I saw lots of M4NK9
(_ _ _ _ _) wearing orange robes.

I ate lots of QZC2 (_ _ _ _) and tried spicy 94UP (_ _ _ _). I wasn't brave enough
though to try the bugs!

THJZ (_ _ _ _) people are really friendly – and they 9MZL2 (_ _ _ _ _) lots! Now I
understand why it's called the LJND 4F 9MZL29 (_ _ _ _ _ _ _ _ _ _ _ _ _)!
I even learned how to say some things – like THJNK Y4U (_ _ _ _ _ _ _ _) and
H2LL4 (_ _ _ _ _).

I think my favorite thing was riding an 2L2PHJNT (_ _ _ _ _ _ _ _ _). But I also
liked 9WZMMZNG (_ _ _ _ _ _ _ _ _) in the 92J (_ _ _). I really liked the exciting
MJQK2T9 (_ _ _ _ _ _ _) too, and the M4UNTJZNS (_ _ _ _ _ _ _ _ _) in Chiang
Mai were pretty neat. I guess I enjoyed 2V2QYTHZNG (_ _ _ _ _ _ _ _ _ _) about
Thailand!

Unscramble these famous places, people, and things from Thailand:

(City)	khuPte	_____	(Person)	gKni	_____
(City)	haCign aMi	_____	(Person)	kMon	_____
(City)	gBaknko	_____	(Animal)	lehapEtn	_____
(Place)	eTlmpe	_____	(Thing)	icRe	_____
(Place)	cheaB	_____	(Animal)	iFhs	_____

Answers: Phuket, Chiang Mai, Bangkok, Temple,
Beach, King, Monk, Elephant, Rice, Fish

And to sum it all up ...

SUMMARY of the trip

We had great fun! What a pity it is over ....

Whom did we meet ...

• Did you meet tourists from other countries? yes / no
  If you did meet tourists, where did they come from?
  (Name their nationalities):

_____

_____

Shopping and souvenirs ...

• What did you buy on the trip?

_____

_____

• What did you want to buy, but ended up not buying?

_____

_____

Experiences

• What are the most memorable experiences of the trip?

_____

_____

_____

_____

A journal

Date   What did we do?

Printed in Great Britain
by Amazon

43878530R00025